HOW WE LEARNED TO SHUT OUR OWN MOUTHS

D1603240

poems

Kathleen Cassen Mickelson

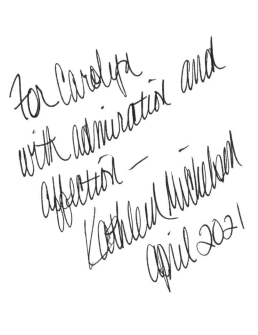

For Carolyn
with admiration and
affection —
Kathleen Mickelson
April 2021

Gyroscope Press

Gyroscope Press
PO Box 1989
Gillette, WY 82717
gyroscopepress@gmail.com

How We Learned To Shut Our Own Mouths
Copyright © 2021 by Kathleen Cassen Mickelson
First Edition 2021

Cover art by Dalsen © 2021
Cover Design, Interior Layout by Constance Brewer

ISBN: 978-1-7367820-0-2

Published in the United States of America

For Mick, my partner in all things,
and my children, Shawn and Abby, who changed
everything.

Foreward

As I write this, the world heaves and cracks. The pandemic that defined 2020 forces us to acknowledge our own fallibility. Here in the United States, we reel not just from the novel coronavirus, but from a polarized population. Deep divisions and wounds never healed keep us on edge, make it difficult to find hope or ease. And yet it is there - hope - if we look hard enough, listen closely enough.

Hope is the place from which this book flows. Much of this year spent at home, tending my own garden, and letting go of anything extra, sharpened the focus of my life. That sharp focus clarified the many reasons for gratitude: my family, my friends, technology that allows us to connect from afar, people who show up for all the necessary jobs that keep us going, and those who show kindness no matter what. I revised my understanding of what is worth fighting for and what must be reckoned with.

Many of these poems were written after my home state of Minnesota shut down to control the spread of the virus. Some were written as Minneapolis rocked with civil unrest in the wake of George Floyd's killing. Some came during the election season, raw with anxiety over whether the results would be what the country needed to keep going forward. These poems pull from what sustains me: my family and the natural world, relationships, and spiritual practice. Those are broad, wide-open, and nebulous ideas, but nothing is off-limits when we are trying to learn how to navigate this world. Nothing is off-limits to the power of love.

And isn't that what art does best? Takes it all in, reassembles whatever "it" is, and presents a new vision?

I have a vision of a world that encourages just that.

Kathleen Cassen Mickelson
December 2020

CONTENTS

HOW WE LEARNED TO SHUT OUR OWN MOUTHS

Notes from the Pandemic

This pandemic invites unhealthy laziness
as I sit with dark thoughts,
wallow in end-of-days scenarios.
Who among us will be dead by next year?
Next month? Tomorrow?

Blank pages in my journal are impossible to fill.
My pen goes back in the too-cheerful polka-dot mug
with other pens, ink gelled in its barrel.

I wrap my arms around my knees,
look out the window to the southwest.
Dark clouds prowl in the distance.
Lightning zits, zaps, strobes.
Faint rumbles narrate the show.

This is what our lives have become:
distant storms, rolling apprehension,
air loaded. Still.

This morning's news talked about
George Floyd's killers, how their body cameras
captured his repeated pleas for breath.
Meanwhile, the US president crows
so many untruths listening to him
is like hearing a child's first work of fiction,
story arc missing, points scattered,
coherence shattered.

Who can work at a time like this?

I'm drawn to my chair, my bed,
irresistible yet comfortless.
When the rain begins, I move
outside, gather drops on my skin,
wish a simple shower did more
than wash away left over grime.

Wedding Anniversary With the World Shut Down

On the morning of our 27th anniversary we cannot make dinner reservations. Steak rests in the refrigerator alongside fresh asparagus scored at yesterday's bi-weekly grocery run. A bottle of wine left by friends last Christmas waits on the kitchen counter.

Later this afternoon, we'll video chat with our kids, all of us hunkered down in front of our laptops at our own dining room tables. This is the hardest part: no hugs from our daughter, son, granddaughter.

My husband gives me a card he made yesterday while I worked. I cry as I read his simple, elegant words. I am supposed to be the poet in this family, goddamn it. All I can do is blubber while he folds his arms around me, my head on his shoulder.

After my last sniffle, we take our time. Cook sausage and eggs, grind coffee beans, boil water, rinse fresh raspberries. There is no reason to rush, nowhere else to be. All we need to do is share this meal, this moment, this now.

On Monday Morning

These roses you gave me Saturday
are still unfolding,
pink and white petals holding their form
in flower yoga, soft but strong,
metaphors for love, for marriage.

I pour myself some coffee, consider how
writing poetry while birds call
and wind chimes sing in the backyard
is a privilege I did not imagine thirty years ago.

Back then, in the throes of single parenthood,
I worried about rent, whether the car would start,
how I would pay for daycare
and when I could earn a big enough paycheck.
What was big enough? Not a secretary's salary.
I wanted the life of an artist with no idea
which dues would pay for me to get there.

When we decided to combine households,
it felt miraculous, undeserved.
We kept our house warm, my son fed,
brought a daughter into the world.
Everything mixed to create a sanctuary
where we could be whatever we wanted.

Here we are.
Monday mornings with music,
poetry, grown children
who have found loves of their own.

Our miracles feel endless
even as our own time grows short.

Hoar Frost

Your light step on the creaky
part of the bedroom floor woke me.
Get up, you said,
you don't want to miss this.
I rolled onto one elbow, looked
at you through tousled hair.

Miss what?

The frost. It's all over everything.
Like a million glass slivers.

I stretched my way to the window, peered out.
Oak branches twisted beneath
glittering frost shards,
in razor-edged relief. I rubbed
my eyes, squinted into
frozen fog, a fairy tale staged
just for us.
Once the sun
rose above the trees,
the tale would end.

I hugged you.

I'm so glad you woke me.

You always know
the right tools
to thaw my heart.

Spring Break at Home

My feet got soaked walking the dogs
on this gray, wet morning while
our daughter slept. She cried last
night. Boyfriend troubles. At 17,
that's the end of the world.

They can't talk clearly to each other.
Sometimes neither can we.
I hate the ache that lodges
in my chest when we argue,
how it presses my heart, pushes
me into sugar binges
and bad poetry.

Those gummy sour candies
on the kitchen counter
are the perfect breakfast
to help me craft this response
that you will never see.

Still

Not a tree limb, not a leaf
moves. Gray light
pregnant with rain
muffles the morning.
A bird twitters and trills
in one of our spruces,
a bird in another yard answers.

I rub the humidity
between my fingers,
inhale warm damp air
as if to cleanse my insides.

There is nowhere I have to be
beyond this table
in front of the patio door,
in view of those still trees
that hold their breath,
wait for the storm.

Practice

Tiger stripe aloeswood beads from last year's visit to
Tassajara Zen Mountain Center ring my wrist. Aloeswood
is said to calm the body, reduce fear and negative energy.
Will it make me less afraid? My fingers rub smooth wood
as I remember stillness. Uncountable stars at night.
Footfalls of the bellringer at 5:20 a.m. to wake us for
meditation. Shoes stacked outside the zendo. Morning
coffee sipped in silence. Meals with people we'll never see
again. Burbles from the creek behind our cabin. The narrow
mountain path to Suzuki Roshi's memorial. How we
learned to shut our own mouths.

Body Count

In this, the summer of fear, the president
does not soothe. He buffets us
with unproven bluster,
broadsides reality.

In this, the summer of face masks,
we barely recognize each other,
empathy submerged when the only faces
we see fully are our own.

In this, the summer of death, the virus
has competition from shots fired
into the backs of Black men
in front of their children.

In this, the summer of our demise,
we still think we'll get what we want.
It's just around the corner.

Hot August Afternoon

A dog barks in a backyard down the street.
Chickadees land on the rain gauge,
chatter a dissonant song, eye the birdbath.
Wind ruffles leaves, scuts clouds
across a hot sky.
Garden dirt crumbles in my fingers.

Flowers look tired. They bow
at the driveway's edge, nod
like drowsy grandparents.
Something builds to the west,
beyond trees, beyond houses.
I feel it push against the afternoon.

Here on the front porch I scribble
words to document these moments
as if I won't remember otherwise,
as if this life ekes out of me
with the waning summer.
My bones still hold me up,
so what is it I think will break
besides my heart
once August ends?

On Labor Day 2020 We Plan Ahead

early September days
looming school terms
the way we marked years with children

our granddaughter prepares for fourth grade
her classroom inside the screen of her first laptop
a new desk beneath her lofted bed
no recess
no noisy line to the school bus
no bumping into friends at lunch

I want to hug her
when she suggests a yoga mat
so she can practice asanas with me via Zoom
I find one in her favorite shade of blue
admire poses printed in white on its surface
wonder how long yoga will hold her interest

I'll show up whenever she asks
as she grows into her own future
mark these years with her
grateful for how loves passes on
how it tingles in fingertips that brush only air

Fall Farmers Market

Splotches of red, green, purple, orange and yellow
Monet together until I put my glasses on,
grocery list in hand, morning air crisp, clear.
Farm trucks form two parallel lines,
back ends facing each other,
tables straining beneath this morning's harvest.

I can't resist the warty pumpkins
even though Halloween is over a month away.
Nor can I pass up perfect purple eggplant,
cherry tomatoes of red and gold,
shiny orange peppers,
earthy inky beets with bits of dirt
still stuck to their skins.

I dream of baba ghanouj, vegetable kebabs,
sheet pans of roasted goodness.
In this moment, pandemics seem far away,
cruelty impossible in the face of such abundance.
All I want is to cook for everyone,
show them the many colors of love.

When Louise Glück Won the Nobel Prize

...she is a human being engaged in the language and in
the world...She's not a person trying to persuade us of
anything, but helping us to explore the world we're
living in. She's a clarifying poet.

- Michael Schmidt of the UK publisher Carcanet
as quoted in The Guardian 10/8/2020

The morning after the 2020 vice presidential debate
we needed something palatable, nourishing,
like toasted English muffins drenched in butter with
raspberry jam
and stories of people who explore
the happiness that sometimes shows up after grief
smoothing a way forward.
What counteracts pandemic fatigue
better than hearing of a woman's success?

Layers of life pile up:
leaves in the backyard,
sweaters folded on the closet shelf,
dishes stacked beside the sink.
We wake each morning still clutching to-do lists
certain that staying busy equals staying well.

I read poems, zero in on layered meanings, wonder
which words I can best wield for myself.
Something niggles beneath the surface.
I let it be, pretend I'm a mystic.
I'm so tired of asking why.

14

Why not give in to whatever spills into
our lives, opens another window with a view
we haven't seen, changes our morning walk route
so much we get lost?
We could open our hands,
welcome that clarity our fear keeps obscured.

October

In the gray of the day
bright gold birch leaves
will not be dimmed.

Chill west wind
makes leaves quiver, dash,
dance along wet curbs.

Autumn's teeth grow sharper,
devour lingering warmth.
The garden dons a coat of dried stalks

while I shrug into a loose sweater,
make tea, consider
what it means to be dormant.

On My Mother's Birthday (haibun)

I wake at 6:00 a.m. so I can be a grandmother to Camille by 7:00 a.m. Out with the dog at 6:30 a.m. Notice the three-quarter moon bright behind quick-bunny clouds, morning stars shining their farewell. Rain-gemmed gold leaves litter the asphalt. So much color in dim light. Sun rises after 7:00 a.m., after Camille knocks on the door, her small hands not strong enough to open the unlocked latch. Pajama-clad, she holds a book in her hands, clothes for the day in a pink plaid backpack. She mumbles *hello Grams*, curls into her favorite chair, still groggy. We keep it quiet. I picture myself in third grade, the last year in the green stucco house on Polk Street. My favorite cold-morning spot was by the furnace vent next to the stove. Warm air rose up under my nightgown, and I, too, held books in my hands: what were they? My mother fermented grape juice into sweet wine in a glass jug she nestled next to the vent. She let me taste it at Thanksgiving. The next summer we moved into a trailer because my parents no longer believed in the American Dream. They whittled our lives to a 10-foot by 54-foot space, breathed relief at less to worry about, and my mother stopped making wine. I stopped sitting next to the stove to warm up. Camille's parents are trying to find a house. I hope Camille finds a special spot in it; I still miss the one I lost.

Your name on my tongue
leaves fall in shifting patterns
spelling cold ahead

After the 2020 Election

We wake the morning after
Election Day, unrested, our night
fitful, our stomachs knotted.
November's newly waning moon
reminds us how shadows move in
before we understand
the light we've lost.

Some say everything is at stake.
That's not always true.
Loss has never been applied
in equal measure.

Today I forgot about the virus.
I can't quite comprehend how,
even as vote counts take
all my attention.

Unseasonably warm weather
pulls me outside, nudges me
along sidewalks, beside lakes.
I sniff the air, think about
what change smells like.
Not soap or exhaust or fresh dog poop,
not cooking odors from the Szechuan restaurant,
or the pine boughs already gathered
for winter décor.

Change? It'll smell like the last thing you expect
so there's no time to reconsider.

Sitting While it Rains

Mick cracks the window so we hear rain
during morning zazen. Chill air tiptoes
into the room, settles around our knees.
Our dachshund snores on her own cushion.

In my head, I am not still.
I think about the poems I'll write,
the FaceTime meeting scheduled for 9:00 a.m.,
how glad I am I can wear
yoga pants all day.

Mick has to go to campus later, collect
horse tissue for research. At least
the horse will be honored by science,
its last contribution on earth.

The rain pings the roof, waters grass
as it dies back before winter.
My gray hair splayed across my shoulders
is evidence I, too, am in the process
of receding from this earth,
any wisdom I have eking into the air.

Waking Early

5:35 a.m. You listen for the dog.
Silence. You wonder if she's dead.
Almost 14, her trachea is slowly collapsing
and walks are not met with eagerness.
She barks at empty chairs.
You expect her demise at any time.

She snorts in her bed next to yours.
You close your eyes, roll over.

6:00 a.m. You're fully awake.
Your husband rose without
you knowing, left
half the bed to cool.

The dog coughs, wheezes, gacks.
You hear her toenails on the wood floor.
You throw back the bed covers,
pull on warm clothes,
get the dachshund-sized harness on the dog,
which reminds you of putting pants on a toddler.

Walking outside in the predawn dark,
you remember why you love
the weeks leading to winter.
The quiet. The smell of snow.
The echo of the crows.
The emptiness of the streets.
You don't mind that the dog
just wants to stand in the front yard.

Back inside, you make coffee.
Not yet 7:00 a.m. You feel like
you've already shared a secret
but aren't sure with whom.
Sunrise may not make anything clearer.
You're not sure you want it to.

A Store of Gratitude

Thursday morning, 7:00 a.m.
My favorite grocery store offers an illusion of safety.
Clean carts, hand sanitizer, everyone masked,
marks indicating where to stand for check out.

This is where panic over an invisible virus choosing its next
        victim
has finally left me, replaced by assessed risk.
Standing several feet from other shoppers,
I examine peppers and potatoes, choose chicken over
        turkey,
reach for Peet's Coffee and Dakota Maid unbleached flour.

I can't see smiles behind required face masks,
but some eyes crinkle as if acquiring groceries brings joy.
And it does. I feel happy as I brush past
holiday displays, aged cheeses, chocolates.

Each well-stocked aisle is a gift.

This place filled with food grown and picked,
washed and sorted, canned and baked, placed
on clean shelves until chosen
is the holiest thing I've experienced in months.

In my head I chant thank you, thank you, thank you.

I stretch my hands toward fresh bread,
eager to unwrap it at my own table,
place it on the tongue of my beloved.

When You Ask Me What I'm Made Of

In this moment, I am made of fallen leaves,
geese v-ing across the sky, early snow.
My heart beats in time to wind that shakes
tree limbs bare. My breath mingles
with pine needles, damp earth,
woodsmoke, plants headed for slumber.
My hair tangles in the North Star,
a veil beneath the full moon.

I am made of owls who hunt
at night, trailing alto hoots along the way.
I am tree frogs on the side of the house,
foxes sneaking into the backyard
to feast on rabbits. There might be
lightning. There might be crickets.

When frost descends, I am made of
flannel shirts, hot coffee, old mittens,
deer tracks around the bird feeder.

I am of the northern seasons, shifting with
the wheel of the year, gear by gear.
I curve to meet the cold.
I lean into winter's crackle.

First Big Snowfall of the Season

Snow cascades into the garden, whitens
pine boughs, loosens the last
birch leaves from their branches.

Gray skies refuse to part for sun or blue beyond.
I shiver inside my sweater, wrap
fingers around my coffee mug.
My face warms in the
hot brew's rising steam.

With nowhere to go, I'm happy
to watch the world transform
to a clean, cold version of itself,
this year's detritus pressed into compost.

Perhaps I'll lock the front door,
put flannel sheets on the bed,
let the weight of them shelter me
until this storm subsides.

The Wild Turkey I Named Lilith

She scratches snow beneath our crabapple,
white flakes gathering on her feathers.
She seems content, if turkeys can feel that way,
pecks at spilled birdseed from our feeder,
eats a bit of stale bread I crumbled there yesterday.
Her silhouette against the winter white morning
makes me happy in that undefinable way
I feel from beings whose language I don't speak.

I worry she's lonely.
Every time I've seen her
no other turkeys gather around.
Once, she flew onto our deck,
eyed us through the patio door,
strutted along the deck rail
with an *I'm a badass* walk.
She assessed our white pines
before flying up to a sturdy branch
to roost for the night.

That was when I named her Lilith,
for her refusal to be subservient to some strutting tom.
Our garden could be her new Eden.

Now she lingers in our front yard
certain we won't harm her.
In the thickening snowfall
Lilith's focus is on food.
Her big feet clear her dirt plate.
She knows how to satisfy her own hunger.

My Poem About Worship

Worship is not a word I use often.
Almost never. I prefer awe.
I prefer love.

Childhood masses were for worship.
The failure of holiness to carry over
to school or elsewhere taught me
to confine adoration within pretty places,
silent places without back talk.

What does it mean to spend all that time kneeling
before that which we neither see nor understand?
To bow before a fairy tale?

It speaks to longing:
a home, love, security.
It speaks to fear
of being left in the cold.

If I let go of all that,
the world opens its petals,
says it was here all along
waiting for me to notice
its intricate web; its multitudes
of conscious beings; its cradles
of ordinary magic in valleys, forests, streams;
its music carried on the wind.
I've learned to accept its invitation,
dig into daily offerings I find
as soon as I step outside,

when I stop trying to control prayer
that seems to appear from nowhere.

This might be what worship reaches for:
the surprise of seeing our own good fortune
encased in dirt we discover on our palms.

Contemplative Season

The full moon slides behind our spruce
through cold morning sky, over grass
sprinkled with frost. I send my breath ahead
in small white puffs, a tiny dragon
setting fire to the world.

December funnels quiet thoughts
as I string tiny bright lights
around our tree. I repeat traditions
not for belief but for comfort.
For love.

My mother, once so precise with lights
and tinsel, is gone 20 years.
We played carols as she died,
hoped she sailed away from us
on melodies she loved.
I finally understand what I carry from her
and grief subsides to allow warmth,
celebration.

As I watch the moon's exit,
early light bathes our backyard,
reflects from our windows,
clears space for winter's raw peace.

Winter Solstice

Dawn raises fingers over the world's edge
while the dog sleeps in the very middle
of the kitchen. I circle to avoid
spilling water for coffee.

She lifts her head, gray fur
rimming her now-alert ears.
Pale sun reaches through the window
to a spot just past her nose.

No one else wakes.
I scratch her neck.

Gray streaks my own hair.
Time tilts toward emptiness
I would rather not claim. Soon
my daughter will leave

breaking open days upon days
of quiet which I cannot yet
imagine embracing.

How to Cook Your Way Out of a Funk

First, turn off the computer. Walk away.
It can't chase you with a knife or throw
a rock at your head. So what if no words
poured onto your screen from your own
hands? Get out of that chair, leave.

Head to the kitchen where it's always warm,
where sustenance is always offered
behind a door or in a drawer.
Grab a purple onion, chop the shit
out of it, throw it into hot olive oil as if
it were the nemesis you most despise.
Once your eyes stop tearing, you'll realize
that heavenly aroma of the onion's
transformation is just the beginning.

Next are those red peppers, that celery. Dice
them into oblivion. Surrender the pieces
to the pan. Mingle in a sprinkle of salt, rub
oregano between your finger and thumb
then let it go. Smash a clove of garlic until
its skin sheds, mince it, shove its pungent bits
into the throng of vegetables.

Feel better? Now, shuffle through those cans
in the cupboard next to the stove. Open
the one with Italian tomatoes, peeled.
Dump it. Stir. Boil water in another pot.
Pasta must make an appearance. Don't forget
to add wine to the first pan,

assuage the vegetables in their heated state.
Lean over the scented steam,
inhale like you mean it.

Step back. You've done what you can.
Find the unopened wine, the red one from Italy,
not that one from California, not this
time. Stab the corkscrew into the cork,
twist, flip, lift. Pour. Sip.
You knew you could create something.

Chickadees in the Birch Trees

Today's doctor appointment did not
cure me of anything. My toes still
fall asleep. I was assured it's merely
a pinched nerve, a strain. Back
exercises should make me stronger.
Resilient.

I remembered an old commitment
to be mindful. I told myself to think
about how I move,
how I express myself,
what I take in.
Was I doing what made me happy?

From my chair, I see chickadees
flit in January-naked birch branches
beneath swollen clouds, swirling flakes.
Their tree-top jig looks like joy.

Gentle Things I Tuck Away Until We Can Gather Again

pink blossoms on Thanksgiving cactus
soft fur on my old dachshund's belly
sunlight illuminating orange squash on the kitchen counter
an old squirrel beneath the bird feeder
      his fur nearly white
rosy gold of a late November sunset
amber glow of Irish whiskey in my glass
Alex Trebek's voice on Jeopardy!
Christmas carols we played as Mom slipped into death
      the back of Dad's neck as he bent to kiss his wife
sonorous saxophone notes as my husband practices
chimes to mark the end of meditation
deer who empty the birdfeeders before dawn
the blue yoga mat on Tuesday mornings
your face on my computer screen
      right here
         untouchable

Acknowledgments

Thank you to *Anti-Heroin Chic* for publishing "My Poem About Worship" and "On My Mother's Birthday" (haibun).

About the Author

Kathleen Cassen Mickelson runs the site, One Minnesota Writer, from her home office in Roseville, Minnesota. Kathleen also co-founded the contemporary poetry journal, *Gyroscope Review*, where she served as co-editor until 2020. She received a BA in English from the University of Minnesota and an MFA in creative writing from Hamline University. When she's not writing, she cooks, hikes with her spouse, takes photos, drinks whiskey, and celebrates her grown children.

Find out more at www.oneminnesotawriter.com

Gyroscope Press
PO Box 1989
Gillette, WY 82717
gyroscopepress@gmail.com

Made in the USA
Columbia, SC
04 April 2021